Horses in Art

DIARY 1987

Published by Alan Hutchison Publishing Co. Ltd.
31 Kildare Terrace, London W2 5JT

The horse, of all animals, is the most impressive to man. 'To witch the wind with cunning horsemanship' was once, as Shakespeare tells us, the ambition of all men, and many artists have tried to 'surpass the life in limning out a well proportion'd steed'. All great paintings of horses also tell us something about both the artist who painted them, and the times in which they were painted. Look, for example, at Ben Marshall's (1767–1835) *Alexandre le Pelletier de Molimede* which brings before us the elegance of rider and mount, the quick, professional movements of the groom, the gloss of the horse's well groomed flanks, and the gleam of boot and saddle. Marshall was artist, sporting journalist and wit. When he decided to quit London and settle in Newmarket, the hub of the racing world, he remarked to his pupil Abraham Cooper 'the second animal in creation is a fine horse, and at Newmarket I can study him in the greatest grandeur, beauty and variety. I have a good reason for going. I discover many a man who will pay me fifty guineas for painting his horse, who thinks ten guineas too much for painting his wife!'.

This famous quip serves as a not inappropriate introduction to this selection of paintings of horses. The earliest date is John Wooton's (1678–1756) savage painting of *Two Stallions Fighting*. Wooton was the first distinguished English sporting painter, whose work can be seen to great advantage in the entrance halls of Althorp and Longleat, where this example hangs, large impressive paintings of hunting scenes in the great estates in which the houses stand. Wooton's contemporary, James Seymour (1702–1752), according to Horace Walpole, 'was thought even superior to Wooton in drawing a horse, but was too idle to apply himself to his profession'. A spendthrift and a gambler who died bankrupt, Seymour's painstaking portraits of horses possess a naive and primitive air of unreality, but in his own day, his work was highly prized for its accuracy.

To pass from Seymour's work to that of George Stubbs (1724–1806) is to enter a far more sophisticated world of pictorial ideas, for it was Stubbs's great achievement to widen the scope of sporting painting in many innovative ways. Amongst his most beautiful works are his classical friezes of *Mares and Foals*, which form his most original contribution to animal painting. Such paintings owed much to the analytical knowledge he gained by dissecting horses, information which he published in 1766 in the remarkable engravings of *The Anatomy of the Horse*. This knowledge also stood him in good stead when painting commissioned portraits of racehorses for exacting and illustrious owners for whom racing had become a major activity. In such works as *The 3rd Duke of Richmond and Family Watching Horses in Training on the Downs*, Stubbs achieves a perfect synthesis between social observation, in the central riding party of the young Duke and Duchess, and action in the rhythmic gallop of the file of hooded, rugged racehorses in bright Goodwood colours of red and yellow.

Something of Stubbs's analytical powers of observation were carried on after his death by the lesser known Swiss born artist Jacques Laurent Agasse (1767–1849), who lived for many years in England, and is seen at his best in his *Two Hunters with a Groom*. The contrast between the cool empiricism of Stubbs and Agasse with the powerful drama of the *Grey Stallion* attributed to the Frenchman Theodore Gericault (1791–1824), provides a telling demonstration of the difference between eighteenth century classicism and early nineteenth century romanticism. The tragically short-lived artist (he died, aged 33 when thrown from a horse) also visited England in 1821 to paint one of the most memorable pictures of the Derby. In all his paintings of horses he used the animal as a dramatic symbol of romantic and untrammeled energy.

With the establishment of the five great classic races for thoroughbred racehorses in the last two decades of the eighteenth century, a demand arose for fine portraits of famous winners, supplied by such specialized artists as Ben Marshall and John Frederick Herring (1795–1865). As a young man Herring was a coachman before becoming particularly associated with the turf, painting no less than 18 winners of the Derby and 33 successive winners of the St. Leger! *Rubini* in the Jockey Club is a fine example of his racing paintings, which were much admired by Degas, the great Impressionist artist also represented in this diary. In his old age Herring retired from the turf, but continued to paint horses in the more domestic setting of the stable in such works as *A Frugal Meal*.

Marshall's most distinguished pupil was the 'Gainsborough of sporting art', John Ferneley (1782–1860), who specialized, not in racing pictures, but in vivid evocations of the hunting field, like *The Birton Hunt*. Ferneley excelled at capturing on canvas the dash of spirited hunters and their elegant riders, their boots gleaming with the gloss of polish made with a mixture of blacking and champagne. Melton Mowbray in Leicestershire was to hunting what Newmarket was to racing. On famous Meltonian was Sir Francis Grant (1803–1878) who after spending a fortune on hunting turned to painting as a career, studied with Ferneley, specialised in equestrian portraits like the charming *Lady Sophia Pelham*, and ended as President of the Royal Academy.

Sir Edwin Landseer (1802–1873), who owned Stubbs's drawings for *The Anatomy of the Horse*, which he left to The Royal Academy, is as an artist more frequently associated with dogs, deer and lions, but his *Arab Stallion* and his Shetland ponies ridden by *The Hon. E.S. Russell and his Brother* show his great powers as a painter of the horse.

Sir Alfred Munnings (1878–1959) was born in Norwich and as a young man lost the sight of one eye when helping a dog out of a thorn bush. But despite this handicap, his relatively little known early paintings of scenes of East Anglian rural life, like *The Ford*, display great sensitivity. Later in life he concentrated on the depiction of fox hunting and racing scenes painted with great panache and understanding. He loved Newmarket Heath, which he immortalised in his splendidly vigorous *Under Starter's Orders*.

Munnings was always a controversial figure, with a gift for a memorable phrase. He once remarked ironically to his friend Lionel Edwards (1878–1966) 'We sporting artists know nothing about art. People who know about horses know nothing about art, and those who know about art know nothing about horses'. In watercolours like *The North Warwickshire*, it was Lionel Edward's unique achievement to depict the very essence of a day across country in the hunting field, not with the old anecdotal humour of the nineteenth century, but with authority and graphic authenticity.

Today, although no longer occupying a central role in daily life, the horse retains its attraction as a pictorial theme to artists as varied as John Skeaping (1901–1980) and Victor Haddelsey (b. 1934). Susan Crawford's (b. 1941) idyllic study of Lipizzaner Mares and Foals portrays some of the future stars of the Spanish Riding School in Vienna, at ease at their stud farm at Lipica in Yugoslavia.

Although commissioned paintings could capture the individual likeness of a great horse for his owner, a demand also existed for portrayals of sporting events amongst a wider public of more moderate means. This demand was supplied by hand-coloured aquatints by artists like Dean Wolstenholme and the Alken family. In their work, the golden age of fox hunting was recorded with immense enthusiasm. The examples reproduced in this diary come from the collection of The British Sporting Art Trust, an independent charity which has as its primary objective the creation and display of a permanent national collection of sporting art. Largely through the Trust's initiative there is now a collection of some fifty paintings at the Tate Gallery, and works are also shown at York City Art Gallery. In 1986 a Gallery of Sporting Art was opened at The National Horse Racing Museum in Newmarket. All these activities need support, and if you are interested in helping with this work, details of Corporate and Individual Membership and of Charitable Giving can be obtained from:

The Organizing Secretary
The British Sporting Art Trust
The Tate Gallery
Millbank, London SW1P 4RG
and
Friends of British Sporting Art
P.O. Box 189
Clifton, Virginia 22024, USA
Lionel Lambourne, Assistant Keeper – Department of Paintings.
Victoria and Albert Museum

DECEMBER 1986/JANUARY 1987

MONDAY 29

TUESDAY 30

WEDNESDAY 31

THURSDAY 1
New Year's Day

FRIDAY 2

SATURDAY 3

SUNDAY 4

The Hon. E.S. Russell and his Brother
Sir Edwin Landseer (1802–1873)
By courtesy of The Iveagh Bequest, Kenwood.

Hon. E. Petre's Bay Filly Matilda with Jockey and Trainer
John Frederick Herring (1795–1865).
Reproduced by kind courtesy of Frost and Reed Ltd.

JANUARY 1987

MONDAY 5

TUESDAY 6

WEDNESDAY 7

THURSDAY 8

FRIDAY 9

SATURDAY 10

SUNDAY 11

JANUARY 1987

MONDAY 12

TUESDAY 13

WEDNESDAY 14

THURSDAY 15

FRIDAY 16

SATURDAY 17

SUNDAY 18

Riding Out
Vincent Haddelsey (b. 1934)

Mares and Foals in a Landscape
George Stubbs (1724–1806)
Tate Gallery

JANUARY 1987

MONDAY 19
Martin Luther King Day (USA)

TUESDAY 20

WEDNESDAY 21

THURSDAY 22

FRIDAY 23

SATURDAY 24

SUNDAY 25

JANUARY/FEBRUARY 1987

MONDAY 26

TUESDAY 27

WEDNESDAY 28

THURSDAY 29

FRIDAY 30

SATURDAY 31

SUNDAY 1

Mr. Russell on his Bay Hunter
James Seymour (1702–1752)
Tate Gallery

The Birton Hunt
John Ferneley Snr. (1782–1860)
Bridgeman Art Library. By courtesy of Christies, London.

FEBRUARY 1987

MONDAY 2

TUESDAY 3

WEDNESDAY 4

THURSDAY 5

FRIDAY 6

SATURDAY 7

SUNDAY 8

FEBRUARY 1987

MONDAY 9

TUESDAY 10

WEDNESDAY 11

THURSDAY 12
Lincoln's Birthday (USA)

FRIDAY 13

SATURDAY 14

SUNDAY 15

Lipizzaner Mares and Foals
Susan Crawford (b. 1941)
Reproduced by permission of the Tryon Gallery

The Right and Wrong Sorts

or a Good and Bad style of going across country

Hunting Sketches
Published by Fores
By courtesy of The British Sporting Art Trust

FEBRUARY 1987

THURSDAY 19

FRIDAY 20

SATURDAY 21

SUNDAY 22

MONDAY 16
Washington's Birthday (USA)

TUESDAY 17

WEDNESDAY 18

FEBRUARY/MARCH 1987

MONDAY 23

TUESDAY 24

WEDNESDAY 25

THURSDAY 26

FRIDAY 27

SATURDAY 28

SUNDAY 1

Persimmon
Emil Adam (1843–1934)
Reproduced by kind permission of the Stewards of the Jockey Club

Mares and Foals Beneath an Oak Tree
George Stubbs (1724–1806)
Reproduced by kind permission of Her Grace, Anne, Duchess of Westminster
Photograph by Geoffrey Shakerly

MARCH 1987

MONDAY 2

TUESDAY 3

WEDNESDAY 4

THURSDAY 5

FRIDAY 6

SATURDAY 7

SUNDAY 8

MARCH 1987

MONDAY 9

TUESDAY 10

WEDNESDAY 11

THURSDAY 12

FRIDAY 13

SATURDAY 14

SUNDAY 15

Match between Aron and Driver at Maidenhead
Richard Roper (c. 1730–c. 1778)
Tate Gallery

The Right and Wrong Sort,

or a Good and Bad stile of going across Country.

London, Published November 1 1890, by MESSRS FORES, Piccadilly.

Drawn by H. Alken.

Engraved by J. Harris.

PLATE 2

Hunting Sketches
Published by Fores
By courtesy of The British Sporting Art Trust

MARCH 1987

MONDAY 16

TUESDAY 17

WEDNESDAY 18

THURSDAY 19

FRIDAY 20

SATURDAY 21

SUNDAY 22

MARCH 1987

MONDAY 23

TUESDAY 24

WEDNESDAY 25

THURSDAY 26

FRIDAY 27

SATURDAY 28

SUNDAY 29

MARCH/APRIL 1987

MONDAY 30

TUESDAY 31

WEDNESDAY 1

THURSDAY 2

FRIDAY 3

SATURDAY 4

SUNDAY 5

APRIL 1987

MONDAY 6

TUESDAY 7

WEDNESDAY 8

THURSDAY 9

FRIDAY 10

SATURDAY 11

SUNDAY 12

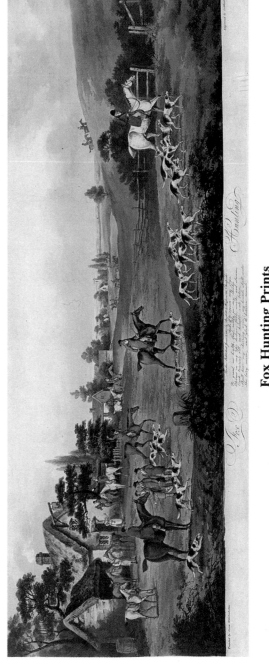

Fox Hunting Prints
engraved by Dean Wolstenholme
Reproduced by courtesy of The British Sporting Art Trust

Brood Mares and Colts in a Landscape
Sawrey Gilpin (1733–1807) and George Barret (1732–1780)
Tate Gallery

APRIL 1987

MONDAY 13

TUESDAY 14

WEDNESDAY 15

THURSDAY 16

FRIDAY 17
Good Friday

SATURDAY 18

SUNDAY 19

APRIL 1987

MONDAY 20
Easter Monday

TUESDAY 21

WEDNESDAY 22

THURSDAY 23

FRIDAY 24

SATURDAY 25

SUNDAY 26

The Duke of Cumberland's Crab
James Seymour (1702–1752)
The Bridgeman Art Library

A Frugal Meal
John Frederick Herring (1795–1865)
Tate Gallery

APRIL/MAY 1987

MONDAY 27

TUESDAY 28

WEDNESDAY 29

THURSDAY 30

FRIDAY 1

SATURDAY 2

SUNDAY 3

MAY 1987

MONDAY 4
May Bank Holiday

TUESDAY 5

WEDNESDAY 6

THURSDAY 7

FRIDAY 8

SATURDAY 9

SUNDAY 10

Lurcher beating Kitt Catt and Ormond 1793
Francis Sartorius (1734–1804)
Reproduced by kind permission of the Stewards of the Jockey Club

Arab Stallion
Sir Edwin Landseer (1802–1873)
Bridgeman Art Library by courtesy of Roy Miles, London.

MAY 1987

MONDAY 11	THURSDAY 14
TUESDAY 12	FRIDAY 15
WEDNESDAY 13	SATURDAY 16
	SUNDAY 17

MAY 1987

MONDAY 18

TUESDAY 19

WEDNESDAY 20

THURSDAY 21

FRIDAY 22

SATURDAY 23

SUNDAY 24

The Right and Wrong Sort,

or a Good and Bad style of going across Country.

Hunting Sketches
Published by Fores
By courtesy of The British Sporting Art Trust

Alabaculia

Benjamin Killinbeck (fl. 1769–1789)

Reproduced by kind courtesy of Frost and Reed Ltd.

MAY 1987

THURSDAY 28

FRIDAY 29

SATURDAY 30

SUNDAY 31

MONDAY 25
Memorial Day (USA)
Late May Bank Holiday

TUESDAY 26

WEDNESDAY 27

JUNE 1987

MONDAY 1

TUESDAY 2

WEDNESDAY 3

THURSDAY 4

FRIDAY 5

SATURDAY 6

SUNDAY 7

Bay Hunter and Grey Arab
George Stubbs (1742–1806)
From the collection at Berkeley Castle
By permission of the Trustee of the Will of the 8th Earl of Berkeley deceased

Lady Sophia Pelham
Sir Francis Grant (1803–1878)
Reproduced by kind permission of Lord Yarborough

JUNE 1987

MONDAY 8

TUESDAY 9

WEDNESDAY 10

THURSDAY 11

FRIDAY 12

SATURDAY 13

SUNDAY 14

JUNE 1987

MONDAY 15

TUESDAY 16

WEDNESDAY 17

THURSDAY 18

FRIDAY 19

SATURDAY 20

SUNDAY 21

Grey Arab belonging to James Henry Legge Dutton, 3rd Baron Sherborne
John Arnold Wheeler (1821–1877)
Reproduced by kind courtesy of Frost and Reed Ltd.

Snake Indians
Alfred-Jacob Miller (1810–1874)
Bridgeman Art Library. By courtesy of Christies, London

JUNE 1987

MONDAY 22

TUESDAY 23

WEDNESDAY 24

THURSDAY 25

FRIDAY 26

SATURDAY 27

SUNDAY 28

JUNE/JULY 1987

MONDAY 29

TUESDAY 30

WEDNESDAY 1

THURSDAY 2

FRIDAY 3
Independence Day Holiday (USA)

SATURDAY 4

SUNDAY 5

The Right and Wrong Sort,

or a Good and Bad style of going across Country.

Hunting Sketches
Published by Fores
By courtesy of The British Sporting Art Trust

Inside a Stable
George Morland (1763–1804)
Tate Gallery

JULY 1987

MONDAY 6

TUESDAY 7

WEDNESDAY 8

THURSDAY 9

FRIDAY 10

SATURDAY 11

SUNDAY 12

JULY 1987

MONDAY 13

TUESDAY 14

WEDNESDAY 15

THURSDAY 16

FRIDAY 17

SATURDAY 18

SUNDAY 19

Spearmint
Emil Adam (1843–1934)
Reproduced by kind permission of the Stewards of the Jockey Club

The Belvoir Hunt. The Meet.
Henry Thomas Alken (1785–1851)
The Tate Gallery

JULY 1987

MONDAY 20

TUESDAY 21

WEDNESDAY 22

THURSDAY 23

FRIDAY 24

SATURDAY 25

SUNDAY 26

JULY/AUGUST 1987

MONDAY 27

TUESDAY 28

WEDNESDAY 29

THURSDAY 30

FRIDAY 31

SATURDAY 1

SUNDAY 2

The Ford
Sir Alfred Munnings (1878–1959)
Reproduced by permission of The Sir Alfred Munnings Art Museum, Dedham

Alexandre le Pelletier de Molimide
Ben Marshall (1767–1835)
Reproduced by permission of The British Rail Pension Fund

AUGUST 1987

MONDAY 3

TUESDAY 4

WEDNESDAY 5

THURSDAY 6

FRIDAY 7

SATURDAY 8

SUNDAY 9

AUGUST 1987

MONDAY 10

TUESDAY 11

WEDNESDAY 12

THURSDAY 13

FRIDAY 14

SATURDAY 15

SUNDAY 16

Jockeys in the Rain
Edgar Degas (1834–1917)
Bridgeman Art Library by courtesy of the Glasgow Art Gallery

Grey Stallion
attributed to Theodore Gericault (1791–1824)
National Gallery of Art, Washington. Collection of Paul Mellon

AUGUST 1987

MONDAY 17

TUESDAY 18

WEDNESDAY 19

THURSDAY 20

FRIDAY 21

SATURDAY 22

SUNDAY 23

AUGUST 1987

MONDAY 24

TUESDAY 25

WEDNESDAY 26

THURSDAY 27

FRIDAY 28

SATURDAY 29

SUNDAY 30

3rd Duke of Richmond and Family Watching Horses in Training on the Downs.
George Stubbs (1724–1806)
From Goodwood House by courtesy of the Trustees

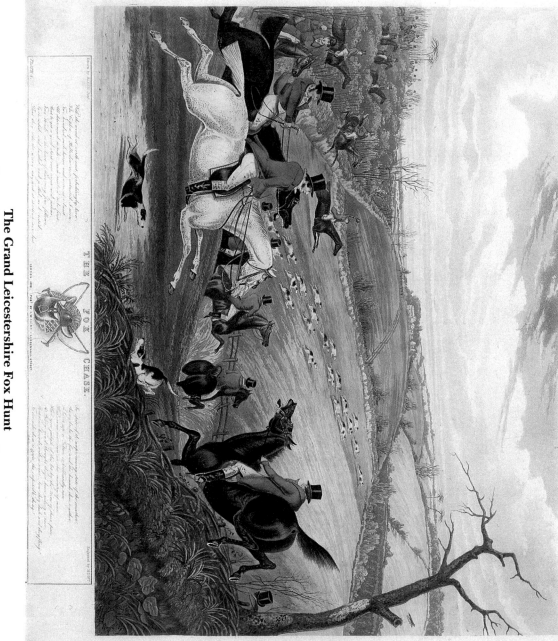

The Grand Leicestershire Fox Hunt

Drawn by Alken Jnr. (1810–1894) Engraved by Hunt

By kind courtesy of The British Sporting Art Trust

AUGUST/SEPTEMBER 1987

MONDAY 31
Summer Bank Holiday

TUESDAY 1

WEDNESDAY 2

THURSDAY 3

FRIDAY 4

SATURDAY 5

SUNDAY 6

SEPTEMBER 1987

MONDAY 7
Labor Day (USA)

TUESDAY 8

WEDNESDAY 9

THURSDAY 10

FRIDAY 11

SATURDAY 12

SUNDAY 13

Birmingham with Conolly Up
John Frederick Herring (1795–1865)
Tate Gallery

Fox Hunting Prints
Engraved by Dean Wolstenholme
Reproduced by courtesy of The British Sporting Art Trust

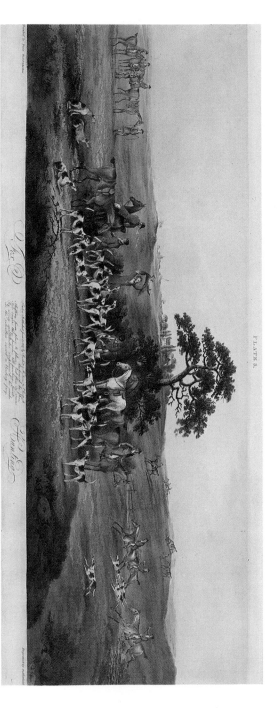

SEPTEMBER 1987

MONDAY 14

TUESDAY 15

WEDNESDAY 16

THURSDAY 17

FRIDAY 18

SATURDAY 19

SUNDAY 20

SEPTEMBER 1987

MONDAY 21

TUESDAY 22

WEDNESDAY 23

THURSDAY 24

FRIDAY 25

SATURDAY 26

SUNDAY 27

Two Stallions Fighting
John Wootton (1678–1756)
By kind permission of the Marquis of Bath

Ormonde
Emil Adam (1843–1934)
Reproduced by kind permission of the Stewards of the Jockey Club

SEPTEMBER/OCTOBER 1987

MONDAY 28

TUESDAY 29

WEDNESDAY 30

THURSDAY 1

FRIDAY 2

SATURDAY 3

SUNDAY 4

OCTOBER 1987

MONDAY 5

TUESDAY 6

WEDNESDAY 7

THURSDAY 8

FRIDAY 9

SATURDAY 10

SUNDAY 11

Two Hunters with a Groom
Jacques-Laurent Agasse (1767–1849)
Tate Gallery

The Grand Leicestershire Fox Hunt

Drawn by Alken Jnr. (1810–1894) Engraved by Hunt

By courtesy of The British Sporting Art Trust

OCTOBER 1987

MONDAY 12
Columbus Day (USA)

TUESDAY 13

WEDNESDAY 14

THURSDAY 15

FRIDAY 16

SATURDAY 17

SUNDAY 18

OCTOBER 1987

MONDAY 19

TUESDAY 20

WEDNESDAY 21

THURSDAY 22

FRIDAY 23

SATURDAY 24

SUNDAY 25

Lord Portmore's Snap Held by Groom with Dog
James Seymour (1702–1752)
Bridgeman Art Library by courtesy of Roy Miles, London.

Horses belonging to Earl Grosvenor
George Stubbs (1724–1806)
Reproduced by kind permission of Her Grace, Anne, Duchess of Westminster
Photograph by Geoffrey Shakerley

OCTOBER/NOVEMBER 1987

MONDAY 26

TUESDAY 27

WEDNESDAY 28

THURSDAY 29

FRIDAY 30

SATURDAY 31

SUNDAY 1

NOVEMBER 1987

MONDAY 2

TUESDAY 3

WEDNESDAY 4

THURSDAY 5

FRIDAY 6

SATURDAY 7

SUNDAY 8

The R.A. Harriers Point-to-Point
Lionel Edwards (1878–1966)
Reproduced by permission of the Tryon Gallery

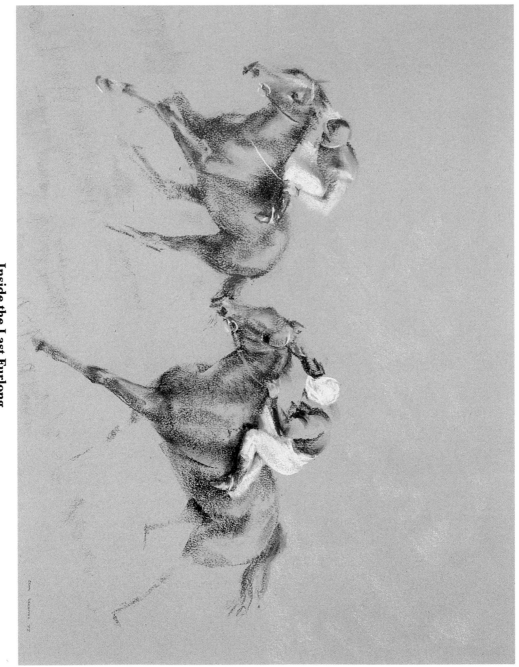

Inside the Last Furlong
John Skeaping (1901–1980)
Photograph by courtesy of Arthur Ackermann and Son Ltd.

NOVEMBER 1987

MONDAY 9

TUESDAY 10

WEDNESDAY 11
Armistice/Veterans Day (USA)

THURSDAY 12

FRIDAY 13

SATURDAY 14

SUNDAY 15

NOVEMBER 1987

MONDAY 16

TUESDAY 17

WEDNESDAY 18

THURSDAY 19

FRIDAY 20

SATURDAY 21

SUNDAY 22

PLATE 1

The Right and Wrong Sort,

or a Good and Bad style of going across Country.

Hunting Sketches
Published by Fores
By courtesy of The British Sporting Art Trust

George IV's Persian Horses Being Taken out for Exercise.
Henry Bernard Chalon (1771–1849)
Tate Gallery

NOVEMBER 1987

MONDAY 23

TUESDAY 24

WEDNESDAY 25

THURSDAY 26
Thanksgiving Day (USA)

FRIDAY 27

SATURDAY 28

SUNDAY 29

NOVEMBER/DECEMBER 1987

MONDAY 30

TUESDAY 1

WEDNESDAY 2

THURSDAY 3

FRIDAY 4

SATURDAY 5

SUNDAY 6

Nothing Stops 'Em
Lionel Edwards (1878–1966)
Reproduced by permission of the Tryon Gallery

Rubini
John Frederick Herring (1795–1865)
Reproduced by kind permission of the Stewards of the Jockey Club

DECEMBER 1987

MONDAY 7

TUESDAY 8

WEDNESDAY 9

THURSDAY 10

FRIDAY 11

SATURDAY 12

SUNDAY 13

DECEMBER 1987

MONDAY 14

TUESDAY 15

WEDNESDAY 16

THURSDAY 17

FRIDAY 18

SATURDAY 19

SUNDAY 20

Under Starter's Orders, Newmarket Start, Cries of "No, No, Sir"
Sir Alfred Munnings (1878–1959)

DECEMBER 1987

MONDAY 21

TUESDAY 22

WEDNESDAY 23

THURSDAY 24

FRIDAY 25
Christmas Day

SATURDAY 26

SUNDAY 27

DECEMBER 1987/JANUARY 1988

MONDAY 28
Boxing Day Holiday

TUESDAY 29

WEDNESDAY 30

THURSDAY 31

FRIDAY 1
New Year's Day

SATURDAY 2

SUNDAY 3

ADDRESSES

NAME	ADDRESS	TELEPHONE

ADDRESSES

NAME	ADDRESS	TELEPHONE

ADDRESSES

NAME	ADDRESS	TELEPHONE

ADDRESSES

NAME	ADDRESS	TELEPHONE

ADDRESSES

NAME	ADDRESS	TELEPHONE

ADDRESSES

NAME	ADDRESS	TELEPHONE

ADDRESSES

NAME	ADDRESS	TELEPHONE

ADDRESSES

NAME	ADDRESS	TELEPHONE

ADDRESSES

NAME	ADDRESS	TELEPHONE

ADDRESSES

NAME	ADDRESS	TELEPHONE

ADDRESSES

NAME	ADDRESS	TELEPHONE

ADDRESSES

NAME   ADDRESS   TELEPHONE

Printed and bound in Hong Kong by South China Printing Co.